D1474554

CARING FOR CHIHUAHUAS MADE EASY

Breed Information, Health Care and Nutrition

By Nadia Alterio,
Founder and Editor of famouschihuahua.com

famouschihuahua.com

Caring for Chihuahuas Made Easy
Breed Information, Health Care and Nutrition
by Nadia Alterio Copyright © 2017

Cover & Interior design by Ramesh Kumar Pitchai

ISBN-13: 978-1544830209
ISBN-10: 1544830203

Table Of Contents

store.famouschihuahua.com
cute chihuahua clothes and accessories

Editor's Note

Who am I? It's simple, a Smart Woman who loves Chihuahuas.

My name is Nadia Alterio and I am the Editor and Founder of FamousChihuahua.com, a fun and informative website that features Chihuahuas and offers helpful Chihuahua information. In 2011, I founded International Chihuahua Appreciation Day celebrated on May 14th by Chihuahua lovers worldwide.

I am also the owner of a Chihuahua named Teaka. In my eyes she is the embodiment of what all Chihuahuas stand for; a source of unconditional love, happiness and a life companion that will always be there for you. She is what inspired me to start Famous Chihuahua®.

Over the years, I have received thousands of emails related to Chihuahua care and health issues. I read every one of them and will continue to do my best to inform people on informative breed facts as well as on how to best care for their Chihuahua. That is why I have put together this book.

The content in this book are for general informational purposes only. They are not meant to be a definitive guide for medical care. If your Chihuahua has a health condition, please bring it to the veterinarian for immediate medical attention under the supervision of

famouschihuahua.com

a professional veterinarian or another health care pet professional.

Chihuahuas are the smallest of the dog breed and within these precious little creatures lays the biggest hearts known to mankind. It is with gratitude that I do what I can through the influence of my site and this book to honour what Chihuahuas stand for worldwide ~ LOVE!

Sincerely,
Nadia Alterio
editor@famouschihuahua.com

SECTION 1: *The Chihuahua*

🐾 Is a Chihuahua the right dog for you?

The Chihuahua, with its apple-head skull and large luminous eyes, can wear a remarkably human expression at times and will want to be with you most, if not all of the time.

Warning: don't buy a Chihuahua if you don't have the emotional real estate in your heart or the time for the complete love and attention of this furry little pet. They are like children.

Chihuahuas can be smooth coat (short haired) or long coat, apple head or deerhead, blue coat or merle coat, there is no Chihuahua breed standard distinction made between the two in the United States, since both smooth coat and long coat can occur in a litter.

The smooth coat Chihuahua has a shorter coat of hair. The hair is fine and needle like. The long haired Chihuahua has a longer coat of hair that usually has a smooth silky like texture. Long haired Chihuahuas are generally smoother to touch and actually shed less hair than the short haired Chihuahua.

Experienced Chihuahua owners say that each dog of this breed has their own unique personality; this is a very individualistic breed.

A few generalizations can be made. Chihuahuas are graceful, energetic, and swift-moving canines. They have often been described as having "terrier-like" qualities; that is, the qualities of being alert, observant, and keen on interacting with their masters. They are extremely loyal and get attached to one or two people.

These tiny and sometimes teacup size dogs are certainly unaware of their diminutive stature: they can be bold with other dogs much larger than themselves, and protective of their masters. They are fiercely loyal to their masters and wary of any strangers or new guests introduced into the household, which the Chihuahua considers to be its personal domain. For these reasons, Chihuahuas make good watch dogs (not guard dogs!).

The Chihuahua needs a great deal of human contact: touching, petting, and general attention. If the Chihuahua does not get this, she or he will use various attention-getting tricks until you give her/him attention. Like using paws to lightly scratch the hand, a signal that says, "pet me now!"

Some owners who have had other, more independent breeds may find the Chihuahua too needy. However, they give a lot of love and affection in return for your care.

Having more than one Chihuahua can greatly ease the dog's stress when left alone each day if the owner works. They will compete for your attention when you get home though. Because they are gentle, loyal, and sweet-tempered, by nature, Chihuahuas are ideal for single people, the elderly, the handicapped, and people who are confined to having to stay inside.

Chihuahuas will keep you company for hours by lying on your lap or beside your torso if in bed, and treat you like royalty. No one with a Chihuahua in his or her household will ever be truly alone. They are quite happy in apartments, as long as there is enough to play with and explore.

Opinions differ on how to bathe a Chihuahua. Some say that bathing too often removes the natural oils from the coat, and thus dandruff will result and the coat will look dull. Others say that shampooing on occasion with certain brands of shampoo can actually enhance the sheen of the coat.

Chihuahuas should be bathed at least twice a month; otherwise they develop an unpleasant smell. This is actually due to the skin cells that human's sloth off onto the Chihuahua, so humans are the main contributors to the smell that can develop.

When bathing Chihuahuas, take care not to get water into their ears, as an infection can develop. You will

famous chihuahua.com

need to trim their nails at least once a month too. On the smaller dogs, cat claw trimmers can be used. It's good to start a nail trimming routine early on, so that your dog becomes accustomed to your handling its paws not to mention getting used to the clippers.

Owners should also be aware that Chihuahuas are prone to knee problems like luxating patellas, or "weak knees." This can happen when they age. If it causes difficulty in walking, take your Chihuahua to the vet.

If a Chihuahua puppy has its American Kennel Club (AKC) official certificate papers, a new puppy can run up to $600.00. The papers, which the breeder provides, mean that the parents of your Chihuahua pup are registered with the AKC and that the puppy is registrable. Toy breeds live the longest of any size dog, so you can expect a lifespan of 11-18 years.

Additionally, some breeders provide pedigree papers, which trace the family history beyond the immediate parents. These papers are vital if you plan to enter your new dog into exhibitions and competitions. These certificates and papers ensure that the dog is a purebred; however, just because a dog has papers, doesn't mean it is any more special than a pup bought from a shelter.

When buying a leash for your Chihuahua, remember that it's neck is rather small and delicate compared to other dog's necks. You cannot (and indeed, should not) yank your dog around by the leash. A body-harness for small dogs is recommended for two reasons: safety and comfort. If fitted right, it will give your Chihuahua a secure and comfortable walk. Harnesses also ensure your dog cannot run into traffic or a bigger creature.

Chihuahuas also prefer several small meals per day, rather than one big meal. They are high-strung dogs. "High-strung" can be defined as: barks easily, does not adapt easily to change in environment, is suspicious of strangers and will growl at them, and flips in circles and jumps around when excited (like when you come home after a five-minute absence, for instance). Your friends will see the worst side of them and never believe you when you tell them that your little buddy is really a gentle, sweet-natured dog.

Are Chihuahuas good with children? Not usually. Owners must be very sensitive to the fact that short haired Chihuahuas, and even long haired ones, are vulnerable to the cold.

In temperatures of 35-40 degrees Fahrenheit, it is recommended that you dress your Chihuahua in a warm dog sweater for brief walks. Walking your Chihuahua in temperatures below 35 degrees Fahrenheit is strongly discouraged, especially when there is a wind-chill factor.

It is characteristic of the Chihuahua to prefer to sleep under a cloth or blanket. They will even get under pillows in order to feel snug. If you are raising a pup, be sure to provide them with a soft towel or blanket in their sleeping area so they can burrow underneath it. Don't be surprised if your Chihuahua scrambles under your blankets at night, even though your house or apartment may not be particularly cold.

Chihuahuas are quite the sun-worshipers. They prefer to bask in the sun for hours and have been known to lie in a spot of sun no larger than the size of a half-dollar! Unfortunately, they are not sensible in this regard and will stay in the sun even when they start to pant.

Watching your Chihuahua in hot weather to be sure that they don't suffer from heat stroke is important. Chihuahuas do shiver when they're cold, but they also shiver when they are wary, excited, unhappy or frightened. This is a result of having a high metabolism, and is a normal characteristic of this breed.

famouschihuahua.com

🐾 Health benefits of Chihuahua ownership

Did you know heart attack patients with Chihuahuas are 8 times more likely to be alive a year later than those without a Chihuahua... and children exposed to Chihuahuas during the first year of life have fewer allergies and less asthma?

Chihuahuas are life companions that provide their owners with unconditional love and acceptance. This devotional trait alone can be of tremendous benefit to our health. The love of a Chihuahua lowers our blood pressure, eases the loneliness that comes with aging or the loss of a loved one and also helps us to overcome allergies.

Calming hormonal changes in the body also occur when we interact with our Chihuahuas. These calming effects help people cope with depression and other stress related disorders. The simple act of petting our Chihuahua actually triggers a release of "feel good" hormones serotonin, prolactin and oxytocin.

Serotonin is a hormone primarily responsible for our mood and prolactin and oxytocin are the two hormones primarily responsible for the production of breast milk. Essentially, a Chihuahua is a great pet if you are suffering from any kind of depressive/anxiety disorder or if you are a new mother or mother to be.

As we pet our Chihuahuas, the levels of our primary stress hormone cortisol decrease. Cortisol is the hormone responsible for proper glucose metabolism, the regulation of blood pressure, insulin release for blood sugar maintenance, immune function and, inflammatory response.

🐾 Chihuahua breed standards

The Chihuahua is the smallest breed of dog in the world and are characterized by the American Kennel Club under the toy group breed which follows these specific show standards:

General appearance - a graceful, alert, swift moving little dog with saucy expression, compact, and with terrier-like qualities of temperament.

Weight - a well balanced little dog not to exceed 6 pounds.

Proportion - the body is off square; hence, slightly longer when measured from point of shoulder to point of buttocks, than height at the withers. Somewhat shorter bodies are preferred in males.

Disqualification - any dog over 6 pounds in weight.

Head - a well rounded "apple dome" skull, with or without molera.

Expression - saucy.

Eyes - full, but not protruding, balanced, set well apart-luminous dark or luminous ruby.

(light eyes in blond or white-colored dogs permissible.)

Ears - large, erect type ears, held more upright when alert, but flaring to the sides at a 45 degree angle when in repose, giving breadth between the ears.

Muzzle - moderately short, slightly pointed. Cheeks and jaws lean.

Nose - self-colored in blond types, or black. In moles, blues, and chocolates, they are self-colored. In blond types, pink nose permissible.

Bite - level or scissors. Overshot or undershot bite, or any distortion of the bite or jaw, should be penalized as a serious fault.

Disqualifications - broken down or cropped ears.

Neck - slightly arched, gracefully sloping into lean shoulders.

Top line - level.

Body - ribs rounded and well sprung (but not too much "barrel-shaped").

Tail - moderately long, carried sickle either up or out, or in a loop over the back, with tip just touching the back. (Never tucked between legs.)

Disqualifications - cropped tail, bobtail.

Forequarters

Shoulders - lean, sloping into a slightly broadening support above straight forelegs that set well under, giving a free play at the elbows.

Shoulders should be well up, giving balance and soundness, sloping into a level back. (Never down or low.) This gives a chestiness, and strength of forequarters, yet not of the "bulldog" chest.

Feet - a small, dainty foot with toes well split up but not spread, pads cushioned. (Neither the hare nor the cat foot.)

Pasterns (Sloping part of foot) - fine.

Hindquarters

Muscular, with hocks well apart, neither out nor in, well let down, firm and sturdy. The feet are as in front.

Coat - in the smooth coats, the coat should be of soft texture, close and glossy. (Heavier coats with undercoats permissible.) Coat placed well over body with ruff on neck preferred, and scantier on head and ears. Hair on tail preferred furry.

In long coats, the coat should be of a soft texture, either flat or slightly curly, with undercoat preferred.

Ears - fringed. (Heavily fringed ears may be tipped slightly if due to the fringes and not to weak ear leather, never down.)

Tail - full and long (as a plume). Feathering on feet and legs, pants on hind legs and large ruff on the neck desired and preferred.

Disqualification - in long coats, too thin coat that resembles bareness.

Color - any color-solid, marked or splashed.

Gait - the Chihuahua should move swiftly with a firm, sturdy action, with good reach in front equal to the drive from the rear.

From the rear, the hocks remain parallel to each other, and the foot fall of the rear legs follows directly behind that of the forelegs.

The legs, both front and rear, will tend to converge slightly toward a central line of gravity as speed increases.

The side view shows good, strong drive in the rear and plenty of reach in the front, with head carried high.

The top line should remain firm and the back line level as the dog moves.

Temperament - alert, with terrier-like qualities.

Other Disqualifications

- any dog over 6 pounds in weight
- broken down or cropped ears

- cropped tail, bobtail
- in long coats, too thin coat that resembles bareness

Source: Official AKC Chihuahua breed standards[1]

Colors and markings of the Chihuahua breed

Chihuahuas are a unique breed that comes in a variety of beautiful colors and markings. The AKC recognizes 29 colors and 11 markings in the Chihuahua breed.

Chihuahuas can be any color, solid, marked, or scattered. Several different color combinations exist and can be found in both short haired and long haired Chihuahuas.

For show purposes, Chihuahuas are classified by type - Standard or Alternate - as well as by a code, which references the registration application for the Chihuahua being shown.

Here are the official colors and markings for the AKC Chihuahua breed standards:

COLORS

Description	Type	Code
Black	S	007
Black & Tan	S	018
Blue & Tan	S	044
Chocolate	S	071
Chocolate & Tan	S	072
Cream	S	076
Fawn	S	082
Fawn & White	S	086
Red	S	140
Black & Red	A	014
Black & Silver	A	016
Black & White	A	019
Black Sabled Fawn	A	354
Black Sabled Silver	A	353
Blue	A	037
Blue & White	A	045
Blue Brindled Fawn	A	356
Blue Fawn	A	036

Chocolate & White	A	271
Chocolate Blue	A	359
Chocolate Brindled Fawn	A	355
Chocolate Sabled Fawn	A	358
Cream & White	A	077
Fawn Brindled Black	A	357
Gold	A	091
Gold & White	A	092
Red & White	A	146
Silver	A	176
Silver & White	A	182
White	A	199

Markings

Description	Type	Code
Black Brindling	S	073
Black Mask	S	004
Black Sabling	S	072
Merle Markings	S	035
Spotted On White	S	071
White Markings	S	014
Black Mask, White Markings	A	005
Blue Mask	A	006

Cream Markings	A	044
Fawn Markings	A	008
Red Markings	A	023

Source: Official AKC Colors & Markings[2]

🐾 Never buy a Chihuahua from a pet store

"If you see a cute Chihuahua puppy in a pet store window, don't buy it!"

Puppies sold at pet stores come from puppy mills!

That's right, we all know about the horrific conditions of puppy mills and how they are the homes of unregulated dog breeding owned by shady breeders, but many people who actually support banishing puppy mills and people who simply want to purchase a Chihuahua don't even know that most pet store puppies come from puppy mills!

If you are reading this and you bought your Chihuahua from a pet store, don't fret. Feel good that you saved a life and consider yourself an amazing person, but please keep the following points in mind if you are going to buy another.

Health problems

Now that you know pet store puppies can come from puppy mills, it's no surprise that these Chihuahuas are going to have health issues. Pet store Chihuahuas are poorly cared for and their parents are not screened for genetic diseases that can be passed onto their offspring.

Common health related issues that can occur include eye problems, teeth problems, genetic deformities, neurological problems and blood disorders.

Behavioural problems

Due to a lack of care and thoughtless breeding practices, behavioural problems are inevitable. Puppy mill breeders don't take the time to ensure potential behavioural issues are weeded out and staff at pet stores is not trained to deal with behavioural issues.

Housebreaking havoc

Chihuahua puppies that are always kept in cages never learn to go to the bathroom away from their food or bed. This can make housebreaking them very challenging and burdensome. Good Chihuahua breeders make a point of keeping their pups in a space that's hygienic and is also providing of a separate area for fecal waste elimination.

Poor socialization

Puppies that are not handled by people at around three weeks of age do not socialize well. Puppy mill breeders usually sell their pups to pet stores when they are far too young, often at only four or five weeks old.

Reputable Chihuahua breeders wait until their puppies are at least 10 weeks old giving them plenty of time to socialize with other siblings in their litter.

Breaking the standard

What you see isn't necessarily what you get. Pet stores ignore AKC Chihuahua breed standards, the guidelines that describe the ideal characteristics, temperament and color and markings of the Chihuahua breed.

You might think you're paying for a genuine purebred Chihuahua puppy with AKC papers, but even if the papers are legitimate, the puppy could still be a flawed representative of its breed. As the puppy grows, you might be surprised to discover your Chihuahua has a little bit of Terrier, Poodle or Jack Russell in it.

Shortage of information

A good Chihuahua breeder is full of information and can tell you all about your pup's family ancestry and specifics like: if your pup is an apple head or deerhead Chihuahua, a blue Chihuahua or even a merle Chihuahua. Pet stores give you very little information regarding family ancestry, potential behavioural issues or health problems.

Little value for what you pay

Pet store Chihuahuas can range anywhere from $200 to $3,000 without after purchase support. There are no laws to protect your purchase from a pet store, but a reputable Chihuahua breeder will guarantee you after care support. This is very helpful for many new Chihuahua owners.

Euthanization

If you bring back a pet store Chihuahua, they are likely to be euthanized. Reputable Chihuahua breeders care about each of their pup's futures and will be concerned about their welfare, so if a problem occurs where the puppy must be returned, rest assured; it will go back to a loving and caring environment.

So if you see an adorable Chihuahua puppy in the window of a pet store, remember that you are probably supporting the horrible practice of puppy mills if you buy it and it's likely health or behavioural issues will result.

Instead, lead by example and support the anti-puppy mill movement. Find a reputable Chihuahua breeder or consider saving a life and adopting your Chihuahua from a local shelter, Chihuahua-specific rescue organization or from a credible puppy mill rescue organization.

famouschihuahua.com

Apple head Chihuahuas vs. deerhead Chihuahuas

What do the terms *apple head* and *deerhead* mean when it comes to describing characteristics of the Chihuahua breed and what exactly makes an *apple head* Chihuahua different from a *deerhead* Chihuahua?

The term *apple head* is used to describe any Chihuahua with a round or 'dome-like' head similar to the shape of an apple. The upper part of the Chihuahua's skull is wider than the lower part in the jaw area.

If you look close at the top of the skull of most Chihuahuas, you will notice that it is slightly sunken in just like the top of an apple. This area is called *molera*, a Spanish word for 'fontanel', or any membranous gap between the bones of the cranium in an infant or fetus and it is similar to the 'soft spot' that human babies have on their heads upon birth.

According to Chihuahua breed standards, the term *applehead* is required in the description of the 'head' of a Chihuahua that includes an apple-domed skull with

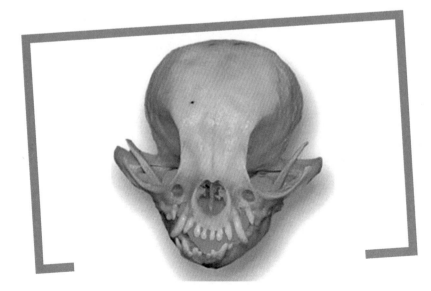

either the presence or absence of *molera*. It is also used when referencing Chihuahua puppies at an age where it is noticeable.

The term *deerhead* is used to describe any Chihuahua that does not have the characteristic apple shaped head. Deerhead Chihuahuas tend to have longer noses and a head shape similar to that of a miniature young deer. They also tend to have less health problems.

Teacup Chihuahuas

What exactly does the term *teacup Chihuahua* mean and is it a legitimate term for characterizing a specific type of Chihuahua? Much controversy exists over this term, so let's get the Chihuahua facts!

The term *teacup Chihuahua* is mainly an American term. It's often used to refer to the size of a Chihuahua and shouldn't be used to categorize a specific type of Chihuahua, as you would reference a short haired vs. a long haired Chihuahua or a deerhead Chihuahua vs. an applehead Chihuahua.

Most Chihuahua puppies are born teacup-sized, but they usually grow out of it when they become adults. In other words, *teacup Chihuahuas* are just very small Chihuahuas usually under 3 lbs in weight and are often called the runts of a litter. They are not a different strain of Chihuahua.

It is important to note that Chihuahuas of this size must be handled delicately and dressed accordingly with the proper clothing to keep them warm and shielded.

famous chihuahua.com

Many prospective Chihuahua buyers are also unaware
of the fact that if a Chihuahua puppy isn't nourished
properly from birth, they will not grow to their full
potential. This undernourishment will keep a Chihuahua
puppy from growing to their full potential as they reach
adulthood.

This is also why it is very important to ask a Chihuahua
breeder what they are feeding their pups and for you
to do your research as to what required nutrients
your Chihuahua will need once you bring them home.
Not all pet food guarantees your Chihuahua proper
nourishment.

Feeding Chihuahuas essential fatty acids from birth
and giving them a vitamin-mineral liquid formula in their

water to ensure they are getting optimal nourishment to grow into a healthy adult is highly recommended. The essential fatty acids are key to a beautiful silky smooth coat.

If a Chihuahua breeder tells you that they breed only teacup Chihuahuas be suspicious, it could be a teacup Chihuahua scam. They are probably seeking a higher price for their puppies.

The terms 'teacup, micro, miniature or pocket size' are just a few of the many labels that have been used by disreputable Chihuahua breeders to lure potential buyers so be sure to research a Chihuahua breeder fully when you are seeking to purchase a Chihuahua and if you are unsure, consider rescuing a Chihuahua instead.

If you are genuinely serious about owning a Chihuahua, the means by which you come to own one shouldn't matter. Also keep in mind, that the smaller the Chihuahua, the more health problems you are likely to encounter.

Is there such a thing as a micro Chihuahua? A pocket Chihuahua?

There is no such thing as a micro Chihuahua or a pocket Chihuahua. Micro-size or pocket Chihuahuas are simply another way of describing teacup-size Chihuahuas. Again, they are usually the runts of a litter and tend to mature with several health problems, have a shorter life span and need more care than the average Chihuahua.

Some even need to be tube fed or bottle-fed until their little bodies are developed enough and they can eat on their own. It is also not uncommon to have to pay daily veterinarian fees to keep these so-called 'pocket or micro Chihuahuas from becoming sick as they age.

It is important to understand that it doesn't mean that Chihuahuas of this size don't deserve love and care, but one can't predict at birth how big a Chihuahua is actually going to get as you don't know if they will experience a growth spurt as they mature.

If a breeder insists that they do know how big their Chihuahuas are going to be, then be leery as this may not be a reputable Chihuahua breeder and is they are probably over pricing their puppies based on false marketing truths with no real research and breeding analysis to base it on.

Knowledgeable breeders will not use terms like 'pocket, micro or teacup' to sell their puppies as they know there is only one Chihuahua breed that ranges in sizes, which vary from 2 to 6 lbs.

On average, most Chihuahuas weigh around 3 to 6 lbs. If they grow to be more or less than this, then that is their fate, but does that mean you will love them any less? If it does, then your reasons for owning a Chihuahua are clearly not genuine. All Chihuahuas, regardless of their size, deserve to be loved and spoiled!

🐾 Blue Chihuahuas

What exactly is a blue Chihuahua and what makes a blue Chihuahua puppy different from other Chihuahua puppies? All Chihuahuas are special and unique in their own way, but blue Chihuahuas are best described as a Chihuahua puppy that is bred to have a dull silver-grey-coat with a tinge of blue.

A blue Chihuahua is rare and can have either apple head or deer head characteristics. They are produced from mating a black and tan Chihuahua, a chocolate, or even a fawn parent, but the parents must carry the recessive blue gene in their line of heritage. The blue in a blue Chihuahua can also be part of a merle patterned, tri-colored or multicolored coated parent.

The Chihuahua Club of America warns that coat color in Chihuahuas is often linked to genes with undesirable traits or birth defects. The merle pattern and blue coat color can often come with health problems - another reason why blue Chihuahuas are rare.

Like teacup Chihuahuas, much controversy exists around the subject of breeding blue Chihuahuas as hidden defects on the gene that is linked to the blue color can result in serious coat problems and other health issues. For these reasons, it is advised to never breed a blue Chihuahua with another blue Chihuahua.

It's unlikely that you'll find a blue Chihuahua in a rescue shelter. In some countries they are highly prized and can cost up to $10,000 depending on their popularity.

Chihuahuas are currently one of the 'hottest' dog breeds in Japan, a country where their fast-growing pet industry is estimated at more than $10 billion a year and pets are fast-replacing having children.

Paying high prices for a Chihuahua with a particular trait is purely the decision of the buyer, but if you're simply looking to give a Chihuahua a nice home, consider adopting one from your local rescue shelter. You might just be surprised to find out that an adopted Chihuahua is the greatest little companion you could have ever dreamed of.

🐾 Merle Chihuahuas

What exactly is a merle Chihuahua and do they carry greater health risks?

Merle Chihuahuas are said to be the latest 'style' or 'designer color' to gain popularity within Chihuahua breeding during the past 15 years, but due to potential health problems, Merle Chihuahuas are also known as *brindle* Chihuahuas and are rarely mentioned in credible books about genetic coloring patterns of the breed.

Chocolate and long haired merle Chihuahuas are also a rare find, thus making them more desirable to people who are more concerned about making a 'fashion' statement.

How does merle breeding work?

The merle gene will change the pigmentation of their base color causing them to have a lighter colored spots throughout their fur coat. Merles can create very intriguing and unique colored Chihuahuas and at times will often have blue eyes.

The merle gene is also a dominant gene. This means that one parent must be a merle for the gene to be passed on to their offspring. Thus the gene will not remain dormant for many years and then suddenly surface.

Are merle Chihuahuas show worthy?

At one time, merle Chihuahuas were eligible for show and were even considered to be purebred by AKC, CKC and KC standards.

famous

However the rules changed as merle Chihuahuas grew less likely to be purebreds and more breeders were just creating mixed breeds with false registration papers. Merle Chihuahuas were also suspiciously increasing in size getting as large as 10 lbs.!

Are merle Chihuahuas more prone to health problems?

The most controversial and debatable issue with merle Chihuahuas is if there exists an increase in potential health problems.

If a breeder does not breed responsibly, then there definitely exists an increased health risk with merle Chihuahuas, but if a breeder breeds responsibly and is credible, merle Chihuahuas are typically happy and healthy just like all other Chihuahuas.

A breeder does not breed responsibly if they mate two purebred merles together, where both parents are merles. In doing so, they think they are strengthening the merle color, but in actual fact they are creating a recipe for disaster as the double merle gene can create Chihuahuas with serious health defects that include blindness, deafness and even severe deformities.

Are there any other health problems in merle Chihuahuas?

Sometimes merle Chihuahuas are sensitive to sunlight when they have the blue eye color, so it's important to keep this in mind when they are outdoors on those bright and sunny days.

So what does all this mean?

Merle Chihuahuas are just as lovable as other
Chihuahuas. It's irresponsible breeding practices that
lead to any major health problems in merle Chihuahuas.
Do your research and ask questions if you are
considering getting a merle Chihuahua and don't be
afraid to investigate the breeder.

Blue Waffle Textured Knitted Sweater
Item code: 1516UPPDWC0

Powder Blue Trench Coat
Item code: 1417UPCM130

Kensington Waterproof Trench Coat
Item code: 1486UPBPVCTC0

Blue Tartan Harness
Item code: 1431UPPHBLT0

Kensington Waterproof Trench Coat
Item code: 1489UPPPVCTC0

Pink Soft Harness
Item code: 1388UPNHUP0

Visit us @ store.famouschihuahua.com

SECTION 2: *Chihuahua Health*

Indications of a 'sick' Chihuahua: When to see a Veterinarian!

Your Chihuahua can't explain its symptoms, so it's your responsibility to keep him or her healthy and to determine whether or not they need veterinary care. Chihuahuas tend to want to hide their illness, so it is up to you to check your Chihuahua for abnormalities.

You know your Chihuahua best, so you will notice subtle early warning signs that someone else might not. If any of the following signs or symptoms of illness exist, call your veterinarian immediately.

Signs and symptoms of a "sick" Chihuahua:

- Lethargy
- Disorientation
- Weakness
- Weight loss
- Seizure
- Lack of appetite
- Vomiting
- Diarrhea
- Unproductive retching, straining to urinate
- Bloody urine
- Difficulty or inability to walk
- Bleeding, pale mucous membranes
- Difficulty breathing and persistent cough

Be prepared: Questions your Veterinarian may ask

Your veterinarian may ask additional questions to help localize or diagnose the problem. It may help to be prepared to answer some of the following questions:

- How long have you owned your Chihuahua?
- Where did you get your Chihuahua (adoption centre, breeder, previous stray)?
- What other type of pets do you have?
- What is the age of your Chihuahua?
- Has your Chihuahua experienced any previous illnesses?
- Is your Chihuahua currently under treatment for an illness or disease?
- What preventative medications is your Chihuahua currently taking?

- Does your Chihuahua receive consistent flea treatment?
- Are any other pets ill?
- Has he/she been vaccinated? If so, when? Which vaccines?
- Have there been any recent pet acquisitions?
- Have there been any recent activities such as boarding, grooming, trip to the park?
- Is a majority of your Chihuahua's time spent indoors or outdoors?
- Have there been any recent changes in diet or eating habits?
- What brand of food, how much and how frequently does your Chihuahua eat?
- What type of table scraps are offered and how frequently?
- What type of treats are offered and how frequently?
- How much water does your Chihuahua typically drink per day?
- Have there been any recent changes in water consumption?
- Have you noticed any coughing or sneezing?
- Have you noticed any lumps or bumps on your Chihuahua?
- Is your Chihuahua urinating normally?
- Is your dog having normal bowel movements?
- When is the last time he/she had a bowel movement?
- Have you noticed any recent weight loss or weight gain?

After answering some general questions, more specific questions need to be answered. A brief exam of your Chihuahua at home can help you determine the answers. These questions are also commonly asked when Chihuahua owners are seeking help over the phone.

Be prepared to answer the following questions, depending on the problem with your Chihuahua:

Regarding the eyes

- Have you noticed an increase or decrease in tear production?
- Do the eyes appear cloudy or red?
- Have you noticed any discharge coming from the eyes?
- Do the eyes appear bloodshot?
- Are the pupils the same size in both eyes?
- Have you noticed your Chihuahua rubbing or pawing at the eyes?
- Is your Chihuahua squinting?
- Do the eyes appear to be sunken or excessively protruding?

Regarding the ears

- Do you notice any swelling or discharge from the ears?
- Are the ears drooping when they normally stand erect?
- Are the ears red and inflamed?
- Do you notice any odour to the ears?
- Is your Chihuahua rubbing or pawing at the ears?
- Have you noticed a lot of head shaking?
- Have you noticed any pain or crying when you rub or scratch your Chihuahua's ears?

Regarding the nose

- Have you noticed any congestion, sneezing or coughing?
- Have you noticed any blood coming from the nose?
- Have you noticed any nasal discharge?

Regarding the mouth

- Have you noticed any swelling of the lips or tongue?
- Have you noticed any bleeding from the mouth?
- What color are the gums - tissue just above the teeth?

Looking inside the mouth

- Are there any foreign objects such as bones or sticks stuck on the roof of the mouth or around the teeth?
- Is your Chihuahua able to open and close the mouth normally?
- Is there any pain involved in opening or closing the mouth?
- Have you noticed any excessive drooling or foaming at the mouth?
- Is your Chihuahua able swallow food normally?

Regarding the chest

- Is your Chihuahua experiencing any difficulty breathing?
- Have you noticed excessive panting?
- Is there any pain when the chest area is petted?
- Have you noticed any recent coughing?
- Is the heartbeat steady and consistent?
- What is the heart rate?

Taking your Chihuahua's heart rate: Place your hand or your ear on the left side of your Chihuahua's chest, just behind the elbow. You should be able to feel or hear the heartbeat. Count how many beats the heart pumps in one minute.

Regarding the abdomen/stomach area

- Has your Chihuahua been having any diarrhea or vomiting?
- Is your Chihuahua able to eat and drink normally?
- Does the abdomen/stomach area appear swollen or distended?
- Does your Chihuahua appear to be in pain when the stomach area is petted?
- Is your Chihuahua known to chew on non-food items such as clothing, towels, rocks, or other items?

Regarding the urinary and reproductive systems

- Have you noticed any difference in urinating?
- Does your Chihuahua seem to strain to urinate or cry in pain?
- Does your Chihuahua repeatedly try to urinate with no urine produced?
- Is there any blood in the urine?
- How frequently does your Chihuahua urinate?
- Is your female Chihuahua spayed?
- Has your female ever had puppies? If so, at what age?
- If your female is not spayed, when was her last heat cycle and was she bred?
- Do you notice any discharge from the vaginal area?
- Is your male Chihuahua neutered? If so, at what age?
- Do you notice any discharge from the penis?
- If your Chihuahua is not neutered, do you notice any swelling of the testicles?
- Have you noticed your Chihuahua excessively licking or grooming the genital area?

Regarding the musculoskeletal system - bones and joints

- Have you noticed any limping?
- Are any legs or joints swollen?
- Has your Chihuahua been excessively licking at one area of his/her legs?
- Does your Chihuahua show signs of pain when walking?
- Is your Chihuahua able to walk normally?
- Does your Chihuahua walk on his/her knuckles?
- Does your Chihuahua drag any legs when walking?
- Does your Chihuahua seem to be in pain when petting him or her?

By supplying the answers to these questions, your veterinarian will be in a much better position to help your Chihuahua. Additional tests may be necessary to find out what the problem is, but the answers to the above questions can greatly narrow the area of concern.

Please note: this information was meant to use only as a guide. If at any time your Chihuahua is exhibiting any of the above signs or symptoms and is showing obvious signs of discomfort, please take them to the veterinarian immediately.

🐾 Tracheal collapse

Chihuahuas are known to suffer from problems related to their soft palate or a collapsed trachea. Tracheal collapse is a condition in which the trachea partially collapses or flattens out as your Chihuahua is trying to breath. This leads to irritation and results in the gagging, coughing and wheezing symptoms.

famouschihuahua.com

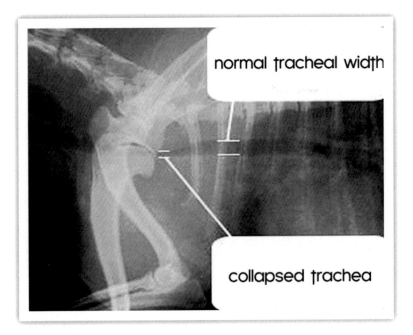

The trachea is the airway from the larynx to the main bronchi in the lungs. It looks somewhat similar to that of a vacuum hose and has many stiff rings with flexible tissue connecting them.

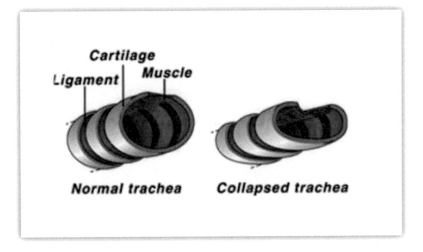

Sometimes these rings are not stiff enough and are unable to hold the trachea open against the air pressure that's created during respiration. The portion of the trachea that is not stiff is then sucked into the airway causing partial obstruction making it difficult for your Chihuahua to breath.

Factors that can lead to tracheal collapse in your Chihuahua are obesity, irritants, allergies, repeated heart conditions, bacterial infections, viruses and second-hand cigarette smoke.

Tracheal collapse can also be brought on by damage done from leash pulling, especially if you use a collar to walk your Chihuahua. It is recommended that you switch to a trachea friendly dog harness to prevent any pushing or pulling against the trachea.

If any of these symptoms develop, take your Chihuahua to the veterinarian right away. If they are not treated, damage can occur in the lungs, larynx, nasal passages and soft palate regions. Your veterinarian will provide you with the right medications and you will be able to prevent further symptoms.

Is snoring related to a collapsed trachea?

Snoring is a common occurrence in Chihuahuas and in most cases is not related to a collapsed trachea, rather it is attributed to their short muzzle and is sometimes it is loud enough to wake the house up. It can be incredibly funny when you have visitors as no one can believe that such a small dog can make that much noise.

Many new Chihuahua owners are amazed the first time they hear the sounds of their Chihuahua enjoying a deep, luxurious sleep. No need to panic, it's perfectly normal and characteristic of the breed. Snoring is something Chihuahua's do when they are relaxed and comfortable.

In fact, Chihuahuas also make snorting and grunting noises when they are playing or just investigating a new smell, which is also perfectly normal.

🐾 Reverse sneezing in Chihuahuas

A classic episode of reverse sneezing might look and sound concerning, but it's usually harmless and often seen in small breed dogs.

What is reverse sneezing?

Reverse sneezing is quite common in Chihuahuas. It is also known as mechanosensitive aspiration reflex, inspiratory paroxysmal respiration, and pharyngeal gag reflex. It is caused by a spasm of the throat and soft palate that is triggered by an irritation to the throat, pharynx, or laryngeal area.

In a regular sneeze, air is pushed out through the nose. In a reverse sneeze, air is pulled rapidly and noisily in through the nose. You might think your Chihuahua is choking or having a respiratory attack, as the sound that occurs with reverse sneezing is sudden and startling.

Typically a Chihuahua will stand still with its elbows spread apart, head extended and eyes bulging as it makes a loud snorting sound that can last anywhere from a few seconds to a couple of minutes.

Common triggers of reverse sneezing:

- excitement
- exercise intolerance

- a collar or harness that's too tight
- pulling on the leash
- environmental irritants like pollen, perfume, household cleaners, room sprays
- a sudden change in temperature

How you can help

It's important to remain calm when your Chihuahua is having an episode or they may become anxious. You can try massaging your Chihuahua's throat or covering its nostrils briefly as this will cause it to swallow which can help clear the irritation and stop the sneezing.

If the episode prolongs, you can try putting your hand in its mouth and pressing on its tongue as this will cause it to open its mouth wider and help move air through its nose.

When to call the vet

Rarely does reverse sneezing require treatment, but if you notice episodes are becoming more frequent, are longer in duration or there's blood or yellow discharge coming from the nose, make an appointment with your vet right away to rule out things like a collapsing trachea, kennel cough, nasal cancer, nasal mites, tumours, or a respiratory infection.

fc

🐾 Kennel cough

What does kennel cough in a Chihuahua sound and look like? How do you know if your Chihuahua has kennel cough? What are the signs of sick Chihuahua with kennel cough and what can you do to treat and prevent it?

Kennel cough is highly contagious respiratory infection caused by the bordetella bacteria and the parainfluenza virus and affects the lungs, windpipe and voice box. These microorganisms attack the lining the respiratory tract causing inflammation. The condition is also known as *tracheobronchitis*.

What are the signs and symptoms of kennel cough?

Look for episodes of high pitched, "honk-like" coughing that lasts for at least 2 weeks, and some Chihuahuas may also vomit up large amounts of phlegm. In order to rid their system of the disease, your Chihuahua needs to cough up phlegm, so don't give your Chihuahua any cough suppressants.

Other than coughing, your Chihuahua will usually not behave sick when it has kennel cough, so limit its activity to avoid triggering intense coughing episodes. If you have other dogs in the house, it is likely they will get kennel cough too.

Try and avoid this by washing your hands after contact with each dog and keeping them separate from each other. Most important, keep your Chihuahua home through the duration of their illness and be sure to give them your loving so they know they are going to be okay.

Although kennel cough is generally not a serious respiratory condition and usually goes away after a few weeks, it is often the case that the cough masks a more serious issue like pneumonia, so it's important to properly care for your Chihuahua to avoid the development of more serious problems.

The key is to carefully monitor your Chihuahua for symptoms so that you can get them checked out as soon as possible.

There is no cure for kennel cough, so prevention is key.

Trips to the dog park with our Chihuahuas can be fun, but it's also a time to be cautious, as it is the place where dogs contract kennel cough most often.

If you plan to board your Chihuahua while you travel, enter them into a dog show, or enrol them into a dog obedience school where there will be a lot of dogs around, it's a good idea to vaccinate your Chihuahua against kennel cough.

Generally, kennel cough vaccines are not necessary for Chihuahuas that stay indoors, so there is greater risk if your Chihuahua is highly socialized with other dogs. There are two kinds of kennel cough vaccines you can get to treat and prevent your Chihuahua.

If you require instant prevention, ask your vet about the intranasal vaccine. It is inhaled through the nose and is best for immediate dog contact situations. The injectable vaccine is the other kind of kennel cough vaccines and can be given to your Chihuahua as early as 4 weeks of age.

famouschihuahua.com

Patellar luxation

The Chihuahua breed is known to have the knee condition known as *patellar luxation* and is one of the most common health problems associated with Chihuahuas.

The knee is a complex structure consisting of muscles, ligaments, tendons, cartilage, and bones. These components must align properly and interact harmoniously in order to function properly. Three bones are included in the knee: the femur, the tibia, and the patella (kneecap).

The lower front portion of the femur (thigh bone) in a normal Chihuahua has two bony ridges that form a fairly deep groove in which the patella is supposed to slide up and down.

These structures limit the movement of the patella to one restricted place, and in doing so, control the activity of the quadriceps muscle. The entire system is constantly lubricated by joint fluid. It works so that there is total freedom of motion between the structures.

Patellar luxation (also known as trick knee, subluxation of patella, or floating patella) occurs when the patella, or kneecap, dislocates or moves out of its normal location.

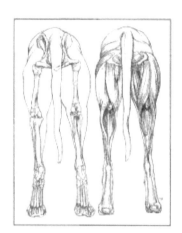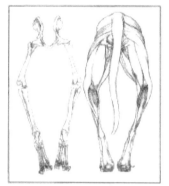

"BOW-LEGGED" STANCE RESULTING
IN MEDIAL PATELLA LUXATION

NORMAL STANCE ON
THE REAR LIMBS

When the patella is luxated in a Chihuahua, the ridges forming the patellar groove are not prominent, and a too-shallow groove is created. In a Chihuahua with shallow grooves, the patella will luxate (jump out of the groove) sideways, especially toward the inside. This can causes the leg to 'lock up' with the foot held off the ground.

When the patella luxates from the groove of the femur, it usually cannot return to its normal position until the quadriceps muscle relaxes and increases in length.

This is why a Chihuahua may be forced to hold their leg up for a few minutes after this occurs because the muscles are contracted, the patella is luxated from its correct position and the joint is held in a flexed or bent position. Pain is caused by the kneecap sliding across the bony ridges of the femur.

Patellar luxation in Chihuahuas can have both genetic causes, and environmental causes (luxation due to injury). If it appears at an early age, it's likely to be due to genetic causes.

Environmental sources of injury can include too much jumping (i.e. jumping off furniture), or too much stress on the patella and surrounding ligaments (i.e. when a Chihuahua dances on its rear legs). This is especially concerning when a Chihuahua is a puppy in stages of early development.

Adult Chihuahuas can also damage their kneecap by a forceful hit or blow. With age, looseness might also be recognized, especially in Chihuahuas that are overweight as there is constant pressure on surrounding ligaments.

Symptoms of patellar luxation includes skipping, yelping when in pain, holding the rear leg up for a short time as they walk or run or rear-leg weakness. If left uncorrected, the condition will result in serious wear of the patellar ridges where the groove becomes very shallow resulting in both arthritis and in the more serious cases, permanent crippling.

If your Chihuahua does have patellar luxation, see your veterinarian for options to help alleviate symptoms. The use of supplements such as glucosamine may be helpful and it's recommended that you keep your Chihuahua lean and exercised to keep the leg muscles strong.

Depending on how severe the condition is, it may or may not require surgery. If required, your Chihuahua should recover quickly. Breeding Chihuahuas with this disorder is not recommended.

The important thing to remember is that Chihuahuas affected still make for wonderful pets and those that do require surgery usually lead perfectly normal lives without any restrictions on activity.

 Joint and paw care

Joint problems in Chihuahuas can range from minor pain and inflammation to more serious conditions such as hip dysplasia, arthritis and rheumatism.

Factors that can cause joint pain are injuries, aging issues, poor nutrition, a lack of exercise, obesity and genetics.

What are the signs of joint problems in your Chihuahua?

The most obvious sign of joint problems is when they are having problems with daily activity. For example, they can't get up on the couch, go up stairs, jump onto the bed and even get up on our laps. They will also tire faster on walks and play for shorter periods of time. They may also hold their limb up or funny while refusing to do activity.

Awkward movements, stiffness, whimpering when getting up or standing, irritability, swelling or thickening of the joints and even refusing to be stroked or petted are also signs of joint problems. It's not that they don't love you; they are simply trying to tell you they are in pain. Do not try to force them to participate in activity as it can worsen problem.

What can you do to prevent injury and help alleviate joint pain?

Pet steps and ramps are will help your Chihuahua get up onto furniture, into bed and in your car. They will once again be able to reach their favourite places without jumping or with human assistance. They are highly recommended for older or Chihuahuas with disabilities.

Pet steps are easy to travel with and prevent us from hurting our own backs when trying to pick up our Chihuahuas. They come in many sizes, materials and fashions, some are heavy duty and others are lightweight.

You can also try natural dog joint care in the form of supplements to help prevent as well as treat pain in the joints and muscles of your Chihuahua.

Caring for your Chihuahua's paws

Winter can be rough on your Chihuahua's sensitive paw pads. It's a good idea to prevent winter weather-related paw pad injuries by following these basic paw care tips to prevent injury:

- When possible, walk your Chihuahua on grass or snow to avoid salty sidewalks. Contact with de-icers can lead to chemical burns.
- Wipe your Chihuahua's paws when they come in from the cold to prevent them from ingesting salty de-icers.
- Trim inner-pad hair from long haired Chihuahuas short during the winter months to prevent ice balls that retain de-icing salts from forming.
- Take your Chihuahua for more frequent short walks to prevent hypothermia or frostbite.
- Feed your Chihuahua essential fatty acids to prevent their skin from cracking or drying out, ...and finally,
- Protect your Chihuahua's paws by having them wear dog booties or paw socks!

🐾 Dry eyes

Chihuahuas tend to have eyes that are more prominent or protruding than other dog breeds, so it's not uncommon for them to develop the eye problem known as *dry eyes*. Dry eyes usually develop in middle-aged or older Chihuahuas and can occur in just one eye or both eyes.

Dry eyes is medically termed *keratoconjunctivitis sicca (kcs)*, which means inflammation of the cornea and surrounding tissues from drying, thus it occurs when the glands of the eye do not produce sufficient tears.

In your Chihuahua's eyes, there are two glands for each eye that provide various components of tears.

famous

If these glands fail to produce enough tears, the eye will become inflamed, which can result in scarring, pigmentation of the cornea, reduced vision or even blindness if left untreated.

Common symptoms and signs of dry eye include:

- redness, irritated eyes
- eyes appear dull, lustreless or dry
- constant blinking
- attempts to paw at the eye
- thick, green discharge
- recurring eye infections or corneal ulcers
- reduced vision

If you notice that your Chihuahua's eyes seem dry or sticky and they have a hard time blinking after they wake up from a nap or a long night's sleep, then there is a good chance they have a dry eye.

If a thick build up of discharge similar to that eye sleep also develops after naps or sleeps, that too is an indicator that they may have a dry eye.

Dry eye may be caused by a number of factors, which include:

- characteristic of dog breed with age
- genetic defects
- inherited abnormalities
- viral infections
- autoimmune conditions
- hypothyroidism
- removal of the third eyelid tear producing gland
- certain drugs such as medications containing sulfa
- anaesthesia
- eye disease or trauma to the eye

Immune-mediated diseases that damage the tear-producing glands is said to be the most common cause of dry eyes. The Chihuahua's immune system attacks the cells that produce a portion of the tear film resulting in a decreased production.

If you suspect your Chihuahua has dry eyes, have your veterinarian do a thorough examination of their eyes and eyelids. They will then be able to properly diagnose your Chihuahua with the condition.

Two tests will be performed. The schirmer tear test, which is a simple test that uses a special wicking paper to measure the amount of tear film produced in one minute, and the fluorescein stain test, which detects corneal ulcers. Additional diagnostic tests may also be performed.

Options for treatment of dry eyes includes the use of eye lubrication or medications that will help to stimulate tear production, replace tears, and reduce inflammation and infection. These include drugs such

famous

as cyclosporine, topical antibiotic eye drops, artificial tear ointments and corticosteroids.

Gentle cleaning of your Chihuahua's eyes several times a day with a warm, wet washcloth will also help your Chihuahua feel better and stimulate tear film production. Always examine your Chihuahua's eyes first thing in the morning and after naps.

You can also apply a gentle saline eye solution to your Chihuahua's eyes periodically to avoid any further discomfort and to keep the eyes clean and free of debris. It's a good idea to keep a bottle handy at all times.

In more severe conditions, a surgical procedure may be performed where a duct from a gland producing saliva is transplanted into the upper lid to replace the aqueous portion of tears. A board-certified veterinary surgeon or ophthalmologist will perform this surgery and is only recommended if all other treatments have failed.

Dry eye is a lifelong condition and requires daily medical care and monitoring of your Chihuahua's eyes, which will mean applying lubricants daily with constant monitoring.

🐾 Shaking puppy syndrome

Shaking Puppy Syndrome is a disease that affects the central or peripheral nervous system of your Chihuahua's brain and is medically termed *hypomyelination*. It's a condition that can occur in all breeds, but it is common in Chihuahuas. The good news is that your Chihuahua puppy can grow out of it and still grow up to live a happy and healthy life.

Puppies that develop the syndrome at birth often are normal. They later develop symptoms at 1 - 2 weeks old. Typically they begin to tremor and it's predominantly more noticeable in the hind legs.

This tremoring can cause them to miss out out on important feedings from their mother as they are less likely to be able to hold their ground when trying to reach their mother's nipples. In these cases, they will require hand feeding.

What causes the shaking?

When an insufficient production of myelin occurs, the substance that insulates and stabilizes nerves, hypomyelination is the result. A lack of myelin causes the nerves to be sensitive resulting in shakes and tremors.

The more active your puppy is, the more they will shake, the less active, the less they will shake. In fact, when they sleep, the shaking often goes away completely.

Other known causes can be related to:

- low blood sugar levels,
- blood birth defects in the vessels of the liver
- and immature brain development

Will your puppy grow out of it?

It depends. If the syndrome has affected their central nervous system, there is a good chance they will grow out of it within a year. If it has compromised their peripheral nervous system, they usually don't get better as they mature. Symptoms usually appear around 5 to 7 weeks when their peripheral central nervous system is affected.

Even though most dogs with the condition grow to have normal lifespans and can participate in most activities that a normal dog would, it is important to recognize that puppies with the condition will likely need help with eating.

Their constant tremoring makes it difficult for them to stand over their food dish to eat. It is also a good idea not to breed these puppies as the likelihood of them passing on the condition to their offspring is high.

🐾 Periodontal disease and obesity

Did you know Chihuahuas can live up to 18 years old if you do two things?

1. Brush your Chihuahua's teeth everyday!
2. Keep your Chihuahua trim and at a healthy weight!

Because Chihuahuas are one of the top dog breeds predisposed to periodontal disease, it is fundamentally important that you brush their teeth every day at the same time if possible to prevent periodontal disease.

Daily teeth brushing can add an extra 2 - 4 years of healthy life to your Chihuahua's expected lifespan.

How does not brushing your Chihuahua's teeth lead to disease?

If your Chihuahuas teeth don't get brushed, food particles and bacteria will collect along the gum line forming plaque. If the plaque is not removed, minerals in the saliva combine with the plaque and form tartar (or calculus), which fixes itself strongly to the teeth.

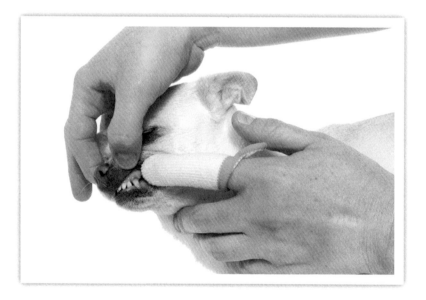

The plaque then starts to mineralize after it forms and the tartar begins to irritate the gums causing inflammation known as *gingivitis,* which is seen as reddening of the gums and causes bad breath. If left untreated, gingivitis will progress to periodontal disease, which is irreversible and can be very painful.

As with adults, dental health care is a key element in the overall health of your Chihuahua. According to the American Veterinary Dental Society, 80% of dogs have periodontal disease by the age of three! This can affect your Chihuahua's internal organs; its heart and can cause pain, which will decrease their quality of life.

The good news is that with regular dental care; you can increase your Chihuahua's life span by two to five years! So start brushing your Chihuahua's teeth if you haven't been doing so already!

How does keeping your Chihuahua thin prevent disease?

Research shows that if your Chihuahua stays at a healthy weight, he or she will live 2 - 4 years longer and old age diseases like arthritis, kidney failure, hypothyroidism and diabetes will either be prolonged or not appear at all.

Obesity is a health concern for these reasons:

- Shortens lifespan
- Leads to diabetes
- Requires a special diet
- Causes joint injuries
- Can trigger tracheal collapse
- Causes lethargy
- Diminishes stamina
- At risk during surgery
- Diminishes immune system
- Leads to digestive disorders

Three signs to tell if your Chihuahua is overweight:

1. If you can't feel their ribs because there's too much body fat.
2. Your Chihuahua has no waistline - they should have an hourglass shaped body when you look down their back.
3. If your Chihuahua's belly bulges out and down when you look at your Chihuahua from the side.

Do your best to keep your Chihuahua at a healthy weight with a nutritious diet and plenty of exercise, as this will save you from costly vet expenses down the road.

Pink Argyle Sweater

Snowman Sweater

Autumn Sweater

Giraffe Print Harness

Active Mesh Neon Red
Harness

Blue Bedtime Pyjamas

Visit us @ store.famouschihuahua.com

famouschihuahua.com

SECTION 3: *Nutrition*

 ## Chihuahuas need EFA's (Essential Fatty Acids)

It is very important to understand that animals and humans share many of the same nutritional and metabolic needs. Certain 'ESSENTIAL' fatty acids obtained through diet are required in both you and your pet for optimal health.

The word ESSENTIAL means just that, essential to the diet because even death can be the result of a severe deficiency in these vital fats.

Whether it be through diet or proper supplementation, it is fundamental that you see to it that both you and your pet are not deficient in these essential life sustaining nutrients.

What are EFAs and how is it that they are 'essential' for your Chihuahua's health?

Realize that Essential Fatty Acids (EFA's) are 'good' fats and will not make your pet fat. Because of their chemical make-up, essential fatty acids are oils. The essential fatty acids Omega-3 and Omega-6, are

vital nutrients that function as necessary building blocks for every cell membrane in your pet's body.

Their liver and other internal tissues do make many of the fatty acids needed that are required for your pet's body's chemical factory to operate normally, HOWEVER with dogs in particular, the one essential fat, Omega-6 (Linoleic acid) CAN NOT be made by their body on its own, so it becomes a MUST for you to see to it that your dog is getting essential fats.

The right amount of essential fats in your dog's diet will help to regulate their cholesterol levels, keep their energy levels up, ensure their immune system is functioning properly and will also alleviate dry itching skin or skin-related conditions.

Essential Fatty Acids also play a vital role in establishing a healthy lipid barrier on the skin of your pet to block any other potential irritants and/ or infections. A consistent intake of the Essential Omega-3 Fatty Acid in sufficient amounts will also help to avoid high blood pressure, reduce the chances of blood clots, and of arrhythmia (an abnormal heartbeat).

Omega-3 also acts as an anti-inflammatory agent by stimulating the production of certain hormone-like substances called prostaglandins.

How do I know if my Chihuahua is deficient in essential fatty acids?

Chihuahuas deficient in essential fatty acids will most likely have easy to detect dermatitis-like characteristics. The best way to assess the possibility an essential fatty acid deficiency in your Chihuahua is to do a thorough inspection of them.

If their skin is dry and flaky and their coat actually feels dull and greasy, but still has a coarse texture, then this is a sure sign that your pet is either not getting any or enough high quality essential fats.

Further defects associated with Essential Fatty Acid deficiencies in your Chihuahua may be one of following:

- eczema, eczema-like skin eruptions
- behavioural disturbances
- dry nose, scratching
- hair loss, gnawing at skin
- arthritis or arthritis-like conditions
- impaired vision or learning abilities
- disrupted healing process
- (wounds are slow to heal or don't heal at all)
- sterility in males
- miscarriages in impregnated females
- hindered growth
- heart and circulatory problems
- drying up of glands, fragility and weakness
- vulnerability to infections
- kidney or liver problems
- coats may have a foul odour
- overall lack of energy

So if your pet has been on a generic, corn-based formula, or on a cheaper "weight-reducing" diet for a long time, or has ANY of the symptoms listed above, then you should re-evaluate your pet's diet and make these much needed changes.

It is very important to look at is the type of dog food you are feeding your pet and the process about which the manufacturer is using to formulate their food.

Usually, the first thing dog food manufacturers will do to formulate a dog food for a "reduced calorie diet" is to cut the total fat content, so there is a reduction of the total calories your pet takes in with each meal. Your pet may or may not lose weight on such a formula, but the potential for an Essential Fatty Acid deficiency is very high.

Make sure your Chihuahua is getting enough essential fats in their diet by having them supplement with a high quality Essential Fatty Acid Oil Blend.

🐾 What dog food is best for your Chihuahua?

There is no one best food for all Chihuahuas. There are so many types and brands on the market so there are hundreds of options and opinions as to which ones are better.

Some Chihuahuas need higher fat and protein than others; some prefer canned over dry food. Feed your Chihuahua what you feel is appropriate for them. It is important to understand that adult Chihuahuas need adult dog food and Chihuahua puppies need puppy food.

If your Chihuahua is from a breeder, ask them what they recommend or if you prefer to ask your Veterinarian, that is fine also, but try not to switch brands too often. With that said, don't be afraid to switch brands if you find one that your Chihuahua does well on.

Use the guaranteed analysis, ingredients listings and feeding guidelines to help make your decision. These guidelines are general, but will give you the recommended amount to be fed based on your Chihuahua's growth level and weight.

Every Chihuahua has a different metabolism, activity level and appetite. Their age and other environmental stresses also impact their daily requirements. Think reasonably and responsibly; if your Chihuahua is thin or hungry, feed it more often and in greater quantity. If your Chihuahua is overweight or obese, feed it less.

🐾 What not to feed your Chihuahua

Chihuahuas are more susceptible to food sensitivities due to their small size. Here is a list of potentially toxic or harmful foods you should avoid feeding your Chihuahua:

- Alcohol
- Avocado
- Chocolate, Coffee and Caffeine
- Tobacco
- Citrus
- Pits (Includes apple cores)
- Coconut and Coconut Oil
- Grapes and Raisins
- Macadamia Nuts

- Milk and Dairy
- Nuts
- Mushrooms
- Onions, Garlic, Chives
- Raw/Undercooked Meat, Eggs and Bones
- Liver
- Salt and Salty Snack Foods (Includes ham)
- Xylitol
- Yeast Dough
- Moldy Foods
- Rhubarb and Tomato leaves (Stems)

Talk to your Veterinarian if you are at all unsure of what to give your Chihuahua. This list is simply helpful information to keep your Chihuahua safe and free of potentially harmful foods.

Source: ASPCA Animal Poison Control Center[3]

References

Chihuahua breed standards

Official AKC Chihuahua breed standards

1. http://akc.org/dog-breeds/chihuahua/

Chihuahua colors and markings

Official AKC Chihuahua colors and markings

2. http://www.akc.org/dog-breeds/chihuahua/detail/

What not to feed your Chihuahua

ASPCA Animal Poison Control Center

3. http://www.aspca.org/pet-care/animal-poison-control

famous

Blue Argyle Sweater

Town & Country Jacket

Blue Snowflake
Knitted Sweater

Red & Black Argyle Sweater

Alpine Hooded Sweater

Green & White Candy
Stripe Sweater

Visit us @ store.famouschihuahua.com

famouschihuahua.com®

Nadia Alterio Biography

Nadia is a former professional athlete, a Psychology graduate, an online marketer extraordinaire, a pet industry writer/blogger and the loving mother of a beautiful young boy.

Her life journey has been nothing short of incredible and she is eternally grateful for the life opportunities that have crossed her path. She currently lives in beautiful Kelowna, British Columbia, Canada, where she runs Famous Chihuahua® and lives each God given day to the fullest.

Nadia dedicates this book to her dearly beloved father, Armando Alterio. His genuine love for their family Chihuahua was undeniably unforgettable.

Fleur-De-Lis Sweater

Pink Bedtime Pyjamas

Butterfly Harness Dress

Plush & Fluffy Terry Bathrobe

Let it Snow "Chilly" Sweater

Red Snowflake
Knitted Sweater

Visit us @ store.famouschihuahua.com

Made in the USA
Middletown, DE
24 July 2017